Tai Chi Chuan's
Internal Secrets

By

Doc-Fai Wong and Jane Hallander

ISBN: 0-86568-
Library of Congress Catalog Card Number: 91-065244

Unique Publications, Inc.
4201 Vanowen Place
Burbank, CA 91505

Edited By: Dave Cater
Designed by: Danilo J. Silverio

Table of Contents

Foreword

Most of the Chinese terms in this book are written in China's standardized *Pinyin* phonetics. Two exceptions are *tai chi chuan* (in Pinyin, *tai ji quan*) and *chi* (in Pinyin, *qi*). Since the public is familiar with them in their previous phonetic spellings, the authors are keeping with those spellings.

However, be aware that the meanings and pronunciation of chi in tai chi chuan and *chi* in chi, the internal energy, are not the same. The outdated Wade-Giles romanizing system used apostrophes to describe pronunciation differences between words – *t'ai chi ch'uan* as opposed to the internal energy *ch'i*. Most apostrophes are excluded in present-day writings, leading to misunderstanding of certain words' actual pronunciation and meaning.

The chi in tai chi chuan means *ultimate*, and is correctly pronounced *jee*. *Chi*, the internal energy, means *air* or *breath*, and is pronounced *chee*.

Chapter One –
The History of Tai Chi Chuan

Tai chi chuan, often phonetically spelled *tai ji quan*, is one of the highest levels of martial art and health practice. *Tai chi chuan* translates to *grand ultimate fist*, referring to what the ancients thought of its benefits.

Today, you can find tai chi in a variety of forms – all named after the families from which they originated. Depending on your preference, your tai chi form may be Chen, Yang, Wu, Sun, Hao or any number of lesser-known styles. Yang family tai chi is the most popular in the world. Chen family tai chi is the current rage among China's wushu stylists and those who like to combine fast and slow movements. While lesser known, the others still have enthusiasts throughout the world.

Originally, tai chi chuan had no family labels. It was simply *tai chi*. Everyone did much the same form and practice. Serious tai chi practitioners started with various meditation postures before ever leaving any moving forms. Moving forms were among the last aspect taught in tai chi.

With a history dating more than 1,500 years, tai chi chuan ranks as one of the world's oldest documented martial arts.

During the Liang period (A.D. 502-557) of China's Northern and Southern dynasty, tai chi already was recorded. One military leader, Cheng Ling-Xi, loved tai chi so much he encouraged his soldiers to practice. In fact, they used its hand-to-hand fighting techniques to successfully defend their military territory. Cheng wrote essays documenting his soldiers' successes to show the martial effectiveness of tai chi chuan.

Several generations later in the Cheng family, Cheng Bi, a scholar of the Imperial Court, wrote that tai chi existed long before his illustrious military ancestor, Cheng Ling-Xi.

During the Tang dynasty (618-907), a martial artist named Xu Xin-Ping also recorded his tai chi knowledge. He called it *tai chi kung*, using the word kung, rather than chuan. Xu learned his martial art from Yu Huan-Zi. The form Xu learned was called the *37 form*, which was similar to Cheng Ling-Xi's century-old tai chi form. Xu handed his

knowledge down to a family named Song. Song Yuan-Qiao, who lived during the Ming dynasty (1368-1644), was the 14th-generation student of Xu.

Song Yuan-Qiao, who was a tai chi student of Zhang San-Feng, wrote a famous tai chi essay, called "Song's Tai Chi Kung." He noted, "People learning now should not forget tai chi's original history. Before my time the people who learned tai chi kung were from the Tang dynasty teacher, Xu Xin-Ping. He handed it down to me through 14 generations. Between those 14 generations, knowledge was lost and rediscovered. Master Xu was from southern China (south of the Yangzi River) from Zi Yang Mountain, Huizhou district, Anwei province. Master Xu lived alone in a hut on the south side of the mountain. His height was 7 feet, 6 inches by ancient Tang measurements. His mustache was down to his naval. His beard was down to his feet. When he walked it was as fast as a running horse. Everytime he carried firewood to the city to sell he sang. Carry the firewood in the early morning to sell, return with the wine in the evening. If you want to know where I live, it is high in the clouds on a green area."

Xu's tai chi kung was named 37 after the number of movements. Since those movements were continuous and flowing, it was also called *chang chuan (long fist)*. Within that early-day tai chi form were some of today's more popular techniques. It included: *wave hands like a cloud; play the fiddle; step forward, parry, punch; single whip; repulse monkey; brush knee, twist step; fair lady works the shuttle; high pat on horse; step up to ride a tiger; grasp bird's tail;* and more.

The resemblance between these and other movements in Xu's form and the modern Yang family tai chi form verifies the age of our own tai chi.

According to Song Yuan-Qiao, when people practiced tai chi, they did only one movement at a time. The 37 form had no beginning or end. It could start from any of its 37 movements. The footwork was designed around the Chinese five elements philosophy—metal, wood, soil, water, and fire.

There was another person in the Tang dynasty who was said to be a tai chi teacher. His name was Li Baozi. He called his tai chi chuan long *fist* or *pre-heavenly fist*.

Today's tai chi got its start during the Mongol-ruled Yuan dynasty (1271-1368) with a scholar named Zhang San-Feng. Zhang gave up his job as a government official to became a recluse and study longevity. He settled in a secluded area of Hua Mountain in Shaanxi province.

3

One day a Taoist priest named Huo Long Zhen Ren (*Fire Dragon Real Man*) visited Zhang. At Zhang's request, the priest took him to his temple to teach him Taoist principles. Zhang learned Taoist longevity health techniques, including tai chi chuan. Zhang eventually moved to Wu Tang (Wu Dang) Mountain, Hubei province, China, where he taught his fledgling tai chi to other Taoists. At the time Zhang studied from the fire priest, he was 67 years old. When he arrived at Wu tang Mountain, he was over 70.

In those days, Taoist priests traveled throughout Chinese countrysides, using their martial arts for self-defense when necessary. Since Zhang already was an old man, he realized he wouldn't stand a chance using conventional martial arts against younger opponents, who are faster and stronger. To equalize his situation, Zhang developed a theory that made him as imposing as any younger enemy. His solution contained four basic principles now an integral part of tai chi chuan. The first principle is to always use *calm* against *action* (calm against excitability). The second calls for using *soft* against *hard* (relaxed against tense). The third principle is *slow* against *fast* (precise against rushed), and the fourth, *single* against a *group* (one technique can defeat many). Zhang said if fighting does not include these four principles, it is not tai chi combat.

The next person in tai chi's lineage was Wang Zong-Yue, a student of a student of Zhang San-Feng. Wang's teacher also was a Taoist priest. Wang Zong-Yue was both a tai chi expert and a scholar writing much about tai chi theory. Branching off from Wang were two tai chi lines, one called the Northern style and the other the Southern style. Northern style tai chi was handed down into the Qing dynasty, during the Kangsi emperor's time (1662-1722), to a man named Jiang Fa.

Jiang Fa made tofu in Xian, Shaanxi province. His mother lived in Hunan. When he made his early visit to Hunan to see his mother, he passed through the Chen family village—Chen Jia Go. Many people in that village practiced *pow chui* (cannon fist), a shaolin-like martial art passed down to the Chen family from the Ming dynasty. Jiang Fa noticed their pow chui movements were stiff and tense. Laughing out loud, he wondered why they needed such brute force. Unfortunately, the Chen village people thought the laughing was an insult to their martial art. Jiang Fa's reaction drew the attention of a strong, muscular man named Chen Chang-Xing (1771-1853). There was a rule then that no one was allowed to make any extra noise when people practiced a martial art. The villagers' reaction told Jiang something was wrong.

Chen Chang-Xing was angry, so he rushed to catch Jiang. He grabbed Jiang's upper arm with one hand. Jiang turned and shrugged off Chen, who tumbled back ten feet to the ground. Chen immediately realized Jiang's superiority. He stood up and bowed, saying, "Master, glad you came." Then he invited Jiang to his home and asked to become one of Jiang's disciples. Jiang, however, was in a hurry to visit his mother. But seeing that Chen was truly sincere, Jiang promised he would return in three years and take Chen as a disciple. Chen asked Jiang what he should practice during those years?

Jiang ordered him to pick up rocks and put them in a pile every morning. Every night he should break off tree limbs and place them in a separate pile. In three years Jiang would be back, expecting to see giant piles. If there were no large pile of rocks and limbs, Jiang would not teach Chen his tai chi fighting.

Chen faithfully followed Jiang's instructions. After three years there were two huge piles of rocks and tree limbs. When Jiang returned he told Chen he had him stack rocks to rid his body of stiffness in his waist and hips. This was caused by too much external practice. Picking the tree limbs was to make Chen's upper body more flexible. Satisfied, Jiang taught Chen tai chi chuan.

The other Chen villagers didn't like Chen Chang-Xing practicing and teaching someone else's martial art, so they forbade him to teach the Chen style pow chui. He only was allowed to teach the outsider's tai chi, mixing it with some of the pow chui movements.

Chen tai chi has changed little through the ages. While new forms have been developed, the style's principles remain the same.

Yang family tai chi, the most popular tai chi style in the world, has its roots with Chen family tai chi chuan.

Yang Lu-Chan (1799-1872) was a native of Hebei province. He and a friend, Li Bai-Hui, brought gifts of money and food for the privilege of studying under Chen Chang-Xing. Yang's long-standing stomach problems would only get better through tai chi's benefits. Li, who had a lung disease, wanted the same benefits. But neither had martial arts in mind when they journeyed to the Chen village. Both men studied diligently for several years, especially Yang, who deciphered many tai chi chuan secrets. When both had completed their training, Li went to

Shaanxi province, where he was invited to teach. He continued to emphasize longevity and health training. Yang Lu-Chan went back to Hebei province, where he had many students.

One of Yang's students, Wu He-Qing (also known as Wu Yu-Shan, 1812-1880) created his own style. Yang Lu-Chan's second son, Yang Pan-Hou, taught Wu most of his tai chi. Wu, who was always stiff and tense, blamed Yang Lu-Chan and his son for keeping all the secrets, instead of admitting he had limited abilities. The result was that Wu left his Yang family teachers to learn directly from Chen Chang-Xing.

Since Chen was 82, he sent Wu to Jao Bao City to study with a relative, Chen Qing-Ping (1795-1868), who taught a tai chi form called *new Chen*. Chen Chang-Xing died the following year. Wu He-Qing studied but one month in Jao Bao. He later wrote he learned every tai chi secret in that one month. He taught tai chi to his nephew, Li Yi-Yu

(1832-1892), who in turn taught Hao Wei-Zhen (1849-1920). The Wu style that Hao learned is sometimes called the Hao style. This is not the same Wu style tai chi practiced today. Hao passed it on to Hao Yue-Ru (1877-1935) and Sun Lu-Tang (1860-1932), who founded today's Sun style.

Yang Lu-Chan took his sons, Yang Ban-Hou (1837-1892) and Yang Jian-Hou (1839-1917), to Beijing and they made Yang family tai chi a big name in local martial arts circles. Yang Jiang-Hou had two sons, the eldest being Yang Shou-Hou, who learned all of the Yang family tai chi secrets and techniques from both his father and uncle. The famous Yang family teacher, Yang Cheng-Fu (1883-1936), was Yang Shou-Hou's younger brother. He learned his tai chi from his father and older brother. Yang Cheng-Fu and his student, Che Wei-Ming, spread tai chi throughout China. Yang Cheng-Fu eventually became the most famous tai chi instructor of modern times. His brother, Yang Shou-Hou, was known as an excellent fighter, but was so rough with his students he never reached Yang Cheng-Fu's popularity.

Meanwhile, three of the emperor's security guards became tai chi disciples of Yang Ban-Hou. All three were Manchurians living in Beijing's Qing dynasty. Their names were Leng Shan, Qian Yo, and Wan Chun. Each received one-third of Yang Ban-Hou's tai chi specialties. Leng Shan learned *gong jing* or hard and strong energy. Qian Yo received the soft dissolving energy called *ro jing*. The third student, Wan Chun, learned *fa jing* or realizing energy.

Learning the soft or ro jing, Qian Yo (1834-1902) taught his son, Wu Jian Quan (1870-1942), who for convenience adopted the surname Wu for teaching tai chi to Han Chinese. Qian Yo is credited as the founder of today's Wu style. He took the original Yang small circle form, also known as fast form, and turned it into the slow, soft, small-circle Wu tai chi style.

However, this book's concern is Yang family tai chi, specifically the form and practice taught by Yang Cheng-Fu.

Yang family tai chi lineage passed down to the authors.

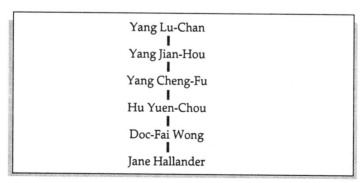

Yang Lu-Chan
|
Yang Jian-Hou
|
Yang Cheng-Fu
|
Hu Yuen-Chou
|
Doc-Fai Wong
|
Jane Hallander

Chapter Two –
Tai Chi's Internal Secrets

Today, everyone first learns the tai chi form, before moving to push hand or maybe token meditation practice. That's not the way the Yang family intended its martial art to be taught. In ancient times, Yang family tai chi teachers didn't start with the form. Students practiced special standing meditation postures and breathing exercises before learning anything else. Each training session began with an hour of standing meditation to build up *chi* (often written *qi).*

Only when their chi was sufficiently developed did they start learning tai chi's martial art *stances.* As they progressed, they eventually combined their training sessions to include meditation, breathing and martial art stances. This lasted for two-to-three years before tai chi *form* position work commenced. Every three months they changed to a different martial art stance, until all 13 positions had been practiced. Some exchanged their tai chi knowledge with xing-yi (hsing-I) and ba kwa (paqua) teachers, adding to the original list of 13. Each posture developed jing (energy) in different parts of the body, while externally strengthening their arms and legs.

After several years, they were taught the tai chi form. However, this was not the connected *moving* form we know today. First they had to stand and hold each technique in the form for 20 breaths. Then they changed to another form posture, repeating the same 20-breath positioning for each posture throughout the entire set.

By practicing the form this way, students learned only one movement at a time. Naturally, it took a long time to finish the entire form. Tai chi students didn't learn to connect form movements until after they had finished memorizing all the postures and their applications. This meant it took several years just to learn the tai chi form. It might have even taken longer, except the Yang long form contains a number of repeat movements.

Meditation, stances and forms postures weren't the only things in a tai chi student's curriculum. Students of Yang family teachers, such as Yang Cheng-Fu, also spent time practicing *tui shou* (push hands). Their push hand practice included single hand, double hand, and something called *ba zhen tui shou* (8 front push hands) that positioned practitioners in stances similar to today's Chen style push hands. Ba zhen eventually became today's Yang style da lu, sometimes called *si zhen si yi* (four front and four corners).

After training for four-to-five years, Yang stylists put their tai chi form into continuous movement. Today, most people practice their form at a very low speed. That wasn't the case in tai chi's early days. Back then, there were two ways to practice the tai chi form. The easiest and most popular was called *zhuo jia*, or *walking the form*. The method practiced by serious students was known a *xing gong*, or *developing the form*. Zhuo jia is done faster than xing gong. It's more like a warm-up form, compared to the chi-developing xing gong method that puts concentration, focus, and intention into a slow, precise form practice. Xing gong is practiced much slower than zhuo jia. Although it takes longer and requires more work, xing gong practice brings greater internal development to tai chi students than the faster, easier zhuo jia method.

At this stage, Yang style tai chi students also practiced actual freestyle sparring with students who attacked with conventional kicks and punches.

It took approximately eight years for Yang family tai chi disciples to complete their training. They learned moving forms and weapons, such as the straight sword, saber, and spear techniques as the last part of their training. Then they practiced on their own.

In later years, Yang Cheng-Fu found that tai chi would never be popular with the general public when taught the old-fashioned way. Most people simply didn't want to devote eight years to what they considered boring training. To keep students interested, Yang opened his teaching with the moving form. Only when students became close students or disciples did they learn the internal side of tai chi training.

Of course, just because Yang Cheng-Fu taught the public tai chi in reverse didn't mean the rest of his family did. His brother, Yang Shou-Hou, and a few other classmates of Yang Cheng-Fu's, still began with the old way of standing meditation

There were more, however, who studied tai chi for its health benefits. This created two branches of Yang tai chi for health. One branch consisted of many of Yang Cheng-Fu's students, who learned the form only for health purposes and called it *tai chi chuan*. The other group learned only the meditation and breathing part of Yang tai chi, but no tai chi form or push hands. They called their branch, *tai chi-chi kung*, now known as *chi kung* (also spelled *qi gong*).

Among those who practiced tai chi only for health reasons, some liked the variety and relaxation of practicing the form. Those were Yang Chen-Fu's everyday students. Others liked the simplicity and

Peng yue, breathing exercise.

lack of need for extra space that the meditations and stance training provided, hence the two ways to practice Yang tai chi for health. Only those students who mastered tai chi for both health and martial arts had everything.

What makes tai chi so beneficial for chi development?

The answer lies in tai chi's most important principles–relaxation and calmness. These are the keys to chi development. Since tai chi is done slow, smooth and even, the result is relaxation. Calmness comes from concentrating on timing, sequence and correct form.

Chi kung is not tai chi. However, it is necessary to master tai chi. Chi kung means chi development and is as simple as meditation and breathing exercises. Meditation requires no movement. It is standing in one place while using a variety of different arm positions. Chi kung meditation requires the body to be totally relaxed *without* external movement. Standing meditations are initially uncomfortable for most students, forcing them to physically relax tense muscles over the one-hour meditation period. Students learn to relax their minds and breathe evenly. Blood circulation starts flowing evenly. This corresponds with the tai chi theory of *silence produces action.*

The other facet of chi kung is its breathing exercises. These include the tai chi form, where the body slowly moves. Proper breathing is a must for relaxation, just as relaxation is critical for good breathing practice. If your breathing isn't even, you won't be relaxed while practicing the tai chi form.

Most people don't realize that under tension or stress, they exhale longer than they inhale. If they are not relaxed while practicing tai chi,

11

their shoulders tense and their breathing rises, throwing off the timing and smoothness of their form. Tai chi breathing exercises teach students to inhale and exhale at the same rate.

Each breathing exercise and meditation posture benefits specific parts of the body, for both health and martial arts. For example, one is good for lowering blood pressure, while simultaneously strengthening the upper arms and shoulders. Another brings the three primary areas of body energy into harmony as it develops *peng jing* or *ward off* fighting energy.

Correct tai chi practice requires both meditation and movement. Standing meditation causes relaxation and develops chi. Movement, including breathing exercises, activates the chi. For instance, the *peng yue* (carry the moon) breathing exercise stirs and balances internal energy. Through its circular pattern, it actually directs energy into the correct parts of the the body by creating a magnetic field from the body movements. After balancing internal energy through the pen yue breathing exercise, the meditation that follows is calm and pure, naturally lowering the body's chi breathing point.

Comprehensive tai chi study must include some internal (chi) training. Without chi development, tai chi would be just another external martial art or exercise. Chi development comes from *passive* meditation and stance training. It must also include chi and physical *activity*, gained from forms practice and breathing exercises.

If you practice tai chi as a martial art, you must also have push hands practice, which requires a partner. You practice forms technique on another person. Tai chi, the martial art, is impossible without two-person practice.

Chapter Three –
Meditation and Breathing
Exercises

Traditionally, there are 13 tai chi meditations and martial art stances, with several extra breathing exercises. In this chapter we talk about tai chi meditation postures and special breathing exercises, which some refer to as *tai chi-chi kung* training.

Daily meditation is the best way to develop better internal power. The standing meditations used by the Yang family forced the body to relax. If students didn't relax during their one-hour meditation period, their shoulders and legs became tense and uncomfortable. Relief came through physical and mental relaxation.

After their bodies relaxed into comfortable postures, their chi started freely moving throughout their bodies. That smoothly flowing chi provided body cells with far more energy-giving oxygen than the average person.

Wu Chi Zhan Zhuang

The first *zhan zhuang*, or standing meditation posture practiced in traditional tai chi schools, is called *wu chi*. While *tai chi* translates to *grand ultimate*, wu chi, often considered the parent of tai chi, means *no ultimate*. It is an emptiness or void, and is the first step toward chi development.

Wu chi zhan zhuang.

Start the wu chi standing meditation with your feet parallel and at shoulder width. Bend your knees as much as possible while remaining comfortable. Keep your back straight and hips slightly tucked. When you place your hand on the small of your back, your lower back should be straight.

Relax your shoulders and chest, making the chest slightly concave. Make sure your body is straight by mentally lining up your navel with your nose. Look straight ahead, focusing far into the distance. Let your arms hang naturally at your sides. Breathe calmly and quietly. Make sure your breathing remains natural.

The middle finger of each hand should touch the center of your thigh where a pressure point called *feng shi* is located. The pressure point at the top of your head, called *bai hui*, should be in a straight line with the *hui yin* point, found directly in front of the anus. A straight line from the hui yin to the ground will be centered midway between the *yong quan* points located at the base of each foot pad.

Now close your eyes.

Wu chi zhan zhuang provides relaxation before the more strenuous standing meditations. It is also the easiest standing meditation for beginners and older people. Because of its relaxing nature, wu chi is a good meditation with which to start. Begin with five minutes of wu chi each day before performing other meditations or stances.

Stand in the wu chi position for ten minutes the first day. Then gradually work up to one hour per day. When you can do the wu chi posture comfortably for one hour, move on to the next level in tai chi meditation.

Tai Chi Zhan Zhuang

The next level of tai chi meditation is known as *tai chi* standing meditation. It begins in much the same way as the tai chi form. With your knees slightly bent, raise both hands–palms facing downward– to shoulder level. Raise your arms only with your shoulder joints. Keep your shoulders relaxed while you raise your arms. Then lower your arms as if you were starting the tai chi form. Each hand is approximately one fist in front and one fist's distance to the side of each thigh. Keep your palms facing down, with your elbows down and slightly bent, and your fingers pointing forward. As you lower your arms, bend your knees as far as possible.

Your eyes should look forward until you are ready for meditation. Then close both eyes. As with wu chi zhan zhuang, mentally line up your navel with your nose. Keep your head straight, as if someone were pulling it by a string from the top of your head. Keep your

shoulders relaxed and chest slightly concave. Your hips should be tucked, with your pelvis pushed slightly forward. This prevents a swayed back. Keep your breathing quiet and natural.

Tai chi standing meditation makes your chi breathing point drop lower into your abdomen. It is a comfortable meditation, because both hands point forward and the circulation flows into the fingers. This prevents the fingertips from getting numb. Bending the knees helps strengthen your leg muscles.

Hun Yuan Zhan Zhuang

The last in the tai chi standing meditation series is called *hun yuan,* or *universe meditation.* Bend both knees and slowly bring your arms up

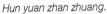
Hun yuan zhan zhuang.

to chest height. Your hands should be rounded with the fingertips pointing toward each other. Keep your hands relaxed and about three-to-four inches apart.

Like the other zhan zhuang meditations, keep your back straight, shoulders relaxed, and your hips tucked. When everything is straight and relaxed, close your eyes.

This particular meditation keeps your chi circulating and connected as it flows from the fingertips of one hand to the other hand and back in a circle. Hun yuan also helps strengthen the arms, developing *peng jing*–ward-off energy.

Tai Chi Breathing Exercises

Tai chi breathing exercises can be done either before or after standing meditation. They develop better blood and chi circulation and calmer breathing patterns. They were developed as quiet combinations for external movements and natural breathing. There are more tai chi breathing exercises than these, however the exercises described here were among the most popular with Yang family disciples.

Peng Yue

Peng yue (holding the moon) is an important tai chi breathing exercise. It balances the energy and creates harmony in what traditional Chinese medical experts call the *triple warmer*.

Triple warmer is a Chinese medical term describing the body's three principle energy areas: the head, controlling upper body energy;

Peng yue zhan zhuang.

16

the torso, representing the body's central portions; and the legs, controlling the lower body energy.

You actually can feel when your triple warmer energy is not balanced. For instance, feeling light-headed or having heavy pressure in your head indicates either not enough or too much energy in that region. Another example is the stomach. If you feel full or empty, no matter how much you have eaten, your torso energy is probably unbalanced. Heavy or light feelings in your legs indicate triple warmer energy is not balanced in the lowest warmer region. The peng yue breathing exercise will help relieve these symptoms and balance the triple warmer.

Start in a standing position, with your feet parallel and spaced a shoulder-width apart. Slightly bend your knees. Your back should be straight, with your buttocks tucked and your pelvis thrust slightly forward. Your shoulders must be relaxed and your chest slightly concave, with the chest muscles relaxed. Do not slouch or round your shoulders too much. Your body should be relaxed. Focus your eyes straight ahead, mentally lining up your nose with your navel.

Starting with your hands at your sides, slowly raise your arms, palms *scooping* upward, in front of your torso. The fingertips of both hands should be pointed toward each other, keeping at least two inches of space between your hands. Raise your hands, palms still in the scooping position, until they are at navel level.

Continue raising your hands, rotating slowly until they are *pushing* upward with your palms facing the sky. Push as far up as you comfortably can. Then slowly pull your hands away from one another, as if your are pulling your fingertips.

Let your hands slowly swing back down in a smooth, even arc until they drop below your *tan tian* (three-fingers width below your navel). Now make a mental connection between the fingertips of both hands, bringing your hands to within two inches of one another. Repeat the process by starting another upward scooping motion.

The key to these tai chi breathing exercises is *natural breathing*. In the case of peng yue, each circle takes too long for an individual breathing cycle, so don't try to time your breathing to each circle. You should be concentrating on your total body connection during the breathing exercise, feeling your internal energy move. Chinese refer to this as *listening to your inside energy*. Repeat each complete peng yue circle 36 times.

Peng yue is excellent for beginning students, since most beginners use only the upper third of their total lung capacity.

Fen Yuan

One of the best chi-developing breathing exercises is fen yuan, or parting the clouds. Start with one foot forward, with your weight resting on your rear leg. Slowly raise your arms, with the palms facing each other at navel height. Still moving slowly, bring your palms to within one inch of each other. Do not let them touch. Then slowly shift your weight forward. Simultaneously push both hands forward until the knee of your front leg lines up with the toe of the same foot. Your arms should be extended, with your elbows slightly bent, making the leg almost straight.

Fen yuan sequence.

At this point, slowly turn your palms down outward and your thumbs downward. With your hands back-to-back, slowly pull them apart until your arms are at 45-degree angles to your body. Now shift your weight over the rear leg. Keep your back straight, with your shoulders relaxed and chest slightly concave throughout this exercise.

When you have shifted your weight directly over your rear leg, slowly turn your palms inward so they are facing. Bring your arms and hands back to the starting position. Repeat the exercise 36 times.

Throughout the fen yuan exercise, look into the distance. Do not focus on anything.

Ye Ma Fen Zhong

Partition the wild horse's mane or *ye ma fen zhong* is a breathing exercise that closely resembles the tai chi form technique bearing the same name. The difference is that when you practice the breathing exercise, you remain stationary.

Start ye ma fen zhong with one foot forward and your weight directly over the rear leg. Hold one arm below your navel, with the palm facing up. The other arm is at midchest height, with the palm facing down, as if you were holding a beach ball.

Ye ma fen zhong sequence.

Movement starts with the bottom hand angling upward to the same hand position as the upper hand in partition the wild horse's mane in the tai chi form. The top hand simultaneously pushes down as if it were doing the form technique. Then the forward hand moves back in a circle to become the top hand. The other hand, which started on the top, makes a circle back, becoming the lower hand.

Shift your weight forward and back with each opening of the rounded hands. Look straight ahead, keeping your back straight and body relaxed. Repeat this exercise 36 times.

21

Dao Juan Gong

Dao juan gong translates to *reverse turning arms*. Like its cousin, ye ma fen zhong, dao juan gong is similar to techniques in tai chi form—*repulse monkey* and *brush knee*.

Start with one foot forward in a brush knee position, with your weight on your back leg. If your left leg is the forward leg, your left hand should be pushing forward. Your right hand will be scooped upward in a repulse monkey position next to your right leg.

Bring your right hand up in a circle next to your right ear and continue forward to the brush knee pushing position. Now turn that same hand, palm upward, as if your were doing repulse monkey, and pull it back to your body–like repulse monkey. At the same time the opposite hand moves forward to a brush knee pushing position. Repeat 36 times, breathing quietly and naturally.

Dao juan gong sequence.

22

With each complete change in hand position, shift your body weight forward and back. With all of the breathing exercises, you can change your leg position halfway through the exercise. Look straight ahead.

If you practice at least one of the meditations one hour a day for 100 days, and supplement these with breathing exercises, you should start feeling chi development. Assuming you are a relatively relaxed person, you should feel heat in the *lao* gong pressure point in the center of your palms. You may also feel tingling in your fingertips. Some individuals even feel the pulse pumping into their hands and into the *yong guan* pressure point at the bottom of the feet. At this time all four pressure points (both hands and feet) are connected by an uninterrupted flow of chi.

Chapter Four –
Tai Chi Martial Stances

Tai chi standing meditations and breathing exercises develop chi. Tai chi forms practice and martial arts stances develop fighting habits.

Realizing that fighting ability takes more than chi development alone, Yang family teachers added focus and intention training to the forms practice. Rather than mindlessly practice the form, tai chi practitioners were taught to visually penetrate an imaginary target. Then, when a real adversary presented himself, tai chi stylists used their relaxed, but still intent, focus against their opponent. This added more penetration to their striking power.

Intention and focus also are important parts of *tai chi stance* training. Don't confuse martial art stances with standing meditation. They are not meditative positions; the eyes are kept open to further a fighting focus and spirit.

Tai chi martial stances are not the same as forms postures. While forms postures represent actual fighting techniques, stances are passive positions that develop specific parts of the body. For instance, the *spear and shield* stance strengthens the upper and lower arm and wrist for future use with the *ward-off* technique.

Tai chi stances also develop a fighting gaze or focus. Unlike standing meditations, the stances are done with eyes looking with purpose into the distance. According to the ancients, a fighter's spirit (*shen*) comes out through his eyes, uniting with his chi to double his strength.

There are ten tai chi fighting stances, each serving a specific training purpose.

Mao Dun

Mao dun translates to *spear and shield*. It resembles a fighter holding a shield in one hand and a poised spear in the other. Place one foot forward in a cat stance position. Your weight should be directly over the other leg. If your have your right foot forward, your right arm will be rounded, with the hand directly in front of you as if holding a shield. Your left arm will be at your side, with the elbow slightly protruding to the rear of your rib cage. The palm of your left or

Mao dun.

spearhand faces your body. The spearhand is held vertical with the fingers pointing straight ahead and the forearm parallel to the ground.

Turn your body sideways, with your chest facing 45 degrees to the left. Look straight ahead without blinking. Quietly breathe. Put your intention on chi coming out of your hand, like a spear thrusting forward, and flowing through the curved arm like a shield repelling an enemy.

Spend ten minutes in this position, then change sides, repeating the stance with your left leg and arm forward. Stay in this position another ten minutes.

Your body, arms and legs should have energy running through them. The force isn't tense, but closer to the soft unyielding energy seen when a garden hose is filled with water. If someone pushes on your arms, you should meet his resistance with *equal* resistance, not force. Do not buckle under his push. Mao dun has several purposes. Besides developing your fighting intention through a relaxed penetrating gaze, the cat stance leg position conditions and strengthens your leg muscles. The forward shield arm is strengthened for future defensive ward-off (peng jing) use. The back or spear arm represents both an offensive elbow strike and forward finger poke. This conditions the muscles in your shoulder, arm, wrist, and hand.

Mao dun's health benefits are the same as all tai chi martial stances. It strengthens your back muscles and ming men pressure point area, completing your upper and lower body connection. You also learn to send tai chi out through your hands, adding more penetration to your strikes and strength to your grabs and jointlocks.

Zheng Shen Pu Hu

At first view, *front body pouncing tiger*, or *zheng shen pu hu*, appears the opposite of its intended purpose. This stance places tai chi practitioners in an uncomfortable, tiring position that forces them to relax their shoulders while strengthening their arms.

Start in a cat stance, with one leg forward and heel raised. Slightly raise both hands above and in front of your head, hands at a 45-degree angle to your wrists, with the palms angled downward. Your upper arms should be level with your shoulders.

Zheng shen pu hu.

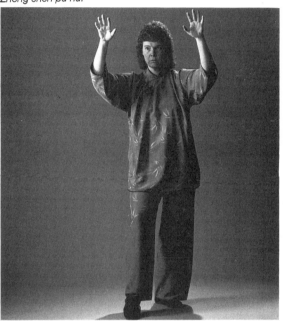

Look straight ahead. Your body should be facing an imaginary opponent, with your hips positioned forward. Stand for ten minutes with one leg forward. Switch to the other leg forward for ten minutes.

The arm muscles strengthened are used for pushing or pressing downward. Your leg muscles also benefit from this stance. As your shoulders relax, chi flows easily into your hands.

Ce Shen Pu Hu

Ce shen pu hu is very close to zheng shen pu hu, except that ce shen pu hu is the *side body pouncing tiger* stance. Instead of strengthening your arms for a front press, ce shen pu hu develops one arm at a time.

Again from a cat stance, if you have your right foot forward, slightly raise and extend your right hand above head level and directly in front of your body. The fingertips are bent into a relaxed position, as if pressing down or pouncing on prey.

The other hand stays in a protective position to the inside of the right hand's elbow. Both hands are at 45-degree angles to their wrists, with the palms down.

Ce shen pu hu.

Unlike the front body pouncing tiger stance, this one has your body at a 45-degree angle to the imaginary target. If your right hand is raised, your body will be angled 45 degrees to the left.

Keep your eyes open and intention focused. Practiced ce shen pu hu for ten minutes daily with each leg forward.

Tuo Ying

Tuo ying, or *lifting the baby*, actually looks as if you are hoisting an infant with both hands. Its benefits are improved wrist flexibility and strength. From a specific martial art standpoint, tuo ying simulates catching someone's leg or arm, with a forward thrust throwing them off balance. Like the other stances, tuo ying also strengthens your legs and relaxes your shoulders.

Tuo Ying.

Start with one leg forward in a cat stance and your body weight resting over the other leg. If your right leg is forward, extend your right arm in front of you, twisting your wrist until your palm is up. Your left arm should be rounded and positioned next to your right elbow, with the hand also twisted up. Turn your waist until your chest faces 45 degrees to the left. It will appear as if you are carefully lifting a baby in front of you.

Look straight ahead with purpose in your eyes. Keep your shoulders relaxed and your back straight. Hold the position for ten minutes on each leg. When you change to left leg forward, extend your left arm out in front, with the right arm by your left elbow.

Zi Wu

Zi wu means *day and night*. It's a stance specifically designed for stretching and loosening joints, such as the hips and knees. You will need a chair for zi wu practice.

Zi wu.

Zi wu is done by placing one foot on top of a chair back or table approximately waist high. If the right foot is on the chair back, the toe points right. Look to the right, with your right hand behind your back and against your ming men pressure point. The palm is outward. The left hand pushes away from your forehead in a protecting position. In the past this stance was done for up to an hour, rotating from leg to leg on the chair or table. Now ten minutes per leg each day is adequate. Besides stretching joints, it helps strengthen leg muscles and improve kicking power.

Lohan Bao Ding

Lohan bao ding, or *arhat carrying an incense burner*, is another tai chi one-legged stance. Lift one foot straight up as high as possible, with the knee bent and the calf of the raised leg parallel to the ground. Turn the toe of the raised foot upward as far as possible. Both arms are evenly rounded and level with the chest, with the fingers pointing toward one another. This makes a connection with your chi.

Lohan bao ding.

Look straight ahead and maintain your balance. When you get tired, change supporting legs. At first, you will have trouble holding each leg for more than 30 seconds. However, if you practice ten minutes a day, you can stand for over four minutes without changing supporting legs.

This stance strengthens the legs and improves balance.

Tui Mo

Tui mo, or *pushing the grinder,* has the feet in a cat stance, with one foot forward and heel raised. Keep your arms level with your waist, with both palms pushing forward. Your fingers should point up with the wrist slightly bent, as if pushing the long handle of a grain grinder. Your elbows point down. Your body and hips should face forward. The distance between both hands is approximately two-and-one-half feet. Again, the eyes look into the distance. Tui mo develops wrist energy from imaginary forward pushing force.

Tui mo.

31

Da Peng Zhan Chi

Da pen zhan chi, which translates to *eagle spread its wings*, starts from a cat stance, one leg forward almost level to the shoulders and extended at a 45-degree angle to the body. Your palms should be facing downward.

The cat stance is used, rather that both feet parallel, to further strengthen the legs. Parallel stances are meditation stances good only for chi development and health. True martial art training requires

Da peng zhan chi.

more difficult cat or one-legged stances. When practicing da pen zhan chi, place your body and hips forward.

Besides conditioning the legs, this stance also strengthens shoulders and arms, while sending chi or energy to fingertips and out the arms. This improves left and right pushing energy.

32

Qing Ting Dian Shui

Qing ting dian shui, or *dragonfly skimming the water*, is done from a cat stance. If your right leg is forward, the right hand is positioned forward and angled upward forehead high, with the palm straight ahead.

Qing ting dian shui.

The left hand pushes to the rear, with the elbow and wrist slightly bent. Look straight ahead, your body at a 45-degree angle to the imaginary target. Relax your waist and chest, focusing your intention into the distance.

Qing ting dian shui develops balanced power on both sides.

Fo Yuan

Floating on top of the cloud, or *fo yuan*, is the only moving tai chi martial stance. From a cat stance with your right leg forward, your right arm will be slightly rounded and extended forward at chest height. Your left arm also is rounded but not extended as far forward as the right. The left arm is held at waist level. Keep both palms down.

Fo yuan.

While looking straight ahead, slightly rock your body forward and backward. Stay relaxed, but be aware of the energy moving your body from side-to-side. This stance develops forward energy and intention. Do it for ten minutes on each side.

Each one of the ten tai chi martial stances requires your lower back be *straight*, not swayed with the hips out. This is critical to your success with any internal system. If you correctly practice these stances with your hips tucked and lower back straight, you eventually will have a strong, naturally connected posture. You will find it hard to be uprooted.

Chapter Five –
The Yang Family Tai Chi Form

Preparation
1   First frame of Yang tai chi form. Feet together, hands at sides.

2   Step out with left foot to a shoulder-width distance.

3   Raise hands to shoulder level.

4   Lower hands to hip level. Bend both knees while lowering hands.

Left ward off
5-6 Turn right 45 degrees, stepping into a left ward off position.

6

7
Grasp bird's tail
Note: the following positions -
ward off, roll back, press and pull
all comprise grasp bird's tail.

Ward off
8-9   Step forward with the right
foot to right ward off position. Left
hand protects at the right elbow.

9

13   Press forward, using the hips
for power.

Push
14   Straighten both arms,
keeping the elbows slightly bent.

15   Draw slightly back.

36

Roll Back
10 Turn waist to right.

11 Using the waist, draw both
hands back 45 degrees to left.

Press
12 Center hips forward, placing
the palm of the left hand against
the pulse of the right arm.

16 Push forward, using hip
power.

Single whip
17 Turn 180 degrees to left.

18 Draw the right hand back to
whip position, with left hand
protecting at the right armpit. Look
in the direction of the whip hand.

19 Step out to single whip. Left hand pushes straight ahead.

Raise hands and step forward
20 Turn 90 degrees to right, right hand raised, left hand opposite the right elbow.

Stork spreads its wings
21 Pull back with both hands, using waist action.

Left brush knee and twist step
25 Turn the right arm inward, palm toward the face. Drop the right hand down while raising the left hand.

26 Raise the left hand to shoulder level.

27 Turn the waist 45 degrees to the right. Right hand circles to a position at ear level.

22 Hands close together, with the right hand protecting the lower body and the left hand protecting the upper body.

23 Step out with the right foot to strike with the right shoulder.

24 Right hand pushes up and to the front. Left hand pushes down.

28 Step forward with left foot. Left hand brushes down over left knee, as right hand pushes forward.

Play the fiddle
29 Shift body weight back to right leg, raising the left toe. Left hand extends forward, with the right hand positioned opposite the left elbow.

Left brush knee and twist step
30 Turn waist 45 degrees to right. Left hand follows waist action. Right hand circles to ear level.

31　Left foot steps forward. Left hand brushes down over left knee, while right hand pushes forward.

Right brush knee and twist step
32　Turn waist 45 degrees to left. Right hand follows waist action. Left hand circles to ear level.

33　Right foot steps forward. Right hand brushes down over right knee, while left hand pushes forward.

Left brush knee and twist step
37　Turn waist 45 degrees to right. Left hand follows waist action. Right hand circles to ear level.

38　Left foot steps forward. Left hand brushes down over left knee, while right hand pushes forward.

Step forward parry and punch
39　Turn waist 45 degrees to left, drawing right fist back. Shift weight to right foot.

40

Left brush knee and twist step
34   Turn waist 45 degrees to right. Left hand follows waist action. Right hand circles to ear level.

35   Left foot steps forward. Left hand brushes down over left knee, while right hand pushes forward.

Play the fiddle
36   Shift body weight back to right leg, raising left toe. Left hand extends forward, with right hand positioned opposite left elbow.

40   Shift weight back to left foot, allowing right foot to take a forward twist step, turning the body 45 degrees to the right. Right fist comes diagonally across the body. Left hand circles to a position level with the left ear.

41   Step forward with left foot as left hand reaches forward in parry position.

42   Punch with right fist, while drawing back left hand to protective position opposite right elbow.

Apparent close-up
43-44   Turn right palm
upward. Left hand slides forward
under right arm.

44

45   Draw back with both palms
facing downward.

Carry tiger to the mountain
49   Turn 45 degrees to right.
Left hand circles to position next
to ear.

50   Step out diagonally with
right foot. Right hand brushes
down over right knee. Left hand
pushes forward.

51   Shift weight to left leg. Right
hand scoops upward.

46 Push forward, using hip power.

Cross hands
47 Turn 90 degrees to right.

48 Close hands, right hand on outside. Feet shoulder's distance apart.

52 Shift weight forward to right leg. Right hand chops diagonally to imaginary opponent's throat.

Diagonal grasp bird's tail
53 Roll back, using waist action.

54 Press forward, placing left palm against right wrist.

55　Straighten both hands.

56　Draw back.

57　Push forward, using hip power.

61　Right foot follows to side. Shift weight to right foot, left toe raised. Left elbow is positioned directly over right horizontal fist.

Right repulse monkey
62　Pick up left foot. Turn left palm upward. Right hand circles to position level with ear.

63　Left foot steps back. Left hand withdraws, as right hand pushes forward.

Fist under elbow
58   Turn 90 degrees to left.

59   Shift weight to right leg, while drawing arms back.

60   Left foot takes a 45-degree twist step.

Left repulse monkey
64   Pick up right foot. Turn right palm upward. Left hand circles to position level with ear.

65   Right foot steps back. Right hand withdraws, as left hand pushes forward.

Right repulse monkey
66   Pick up left foot. Turn left palm upward. Right hand circles to position level with ear.

67 Left foot steps back. Left hand withdraws, as right hand pushes forward.

Slanting Flying
68 Turn 90 degrees to right. Right hand scooped under left hand.

69 Step out with right foot. Right hand extends forward.

73 Step out with right foot into a right shoulder strike.

74 Right hand pushes up and to the front. Left hand pushes down. Pick up left foot, replacing it with the toe down.

Left brush knee and twist step
75 Turn right arm inward, palm toward the face. Lower right hand, while raising left hand.

Raise hands and step forward
70 Shift weight back to left leg.
Right arm extends forward. Left
hand positioned opposite right
elbow.

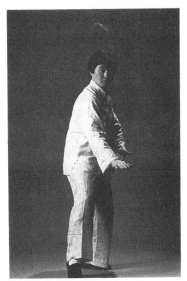

71 Pull back with both hands,
using waist action.

72 Scoop under, right hand
protecting lower body and left
hand protecting upper body.

76 Raise left hand to shoulder
level. Turn waist 45 degrees to
right. Left hand follows direction
of waist. Right hand circles to
position at ear level.

77 Step forward with left foot.
Left hand brushes down over left
knee, as right hand pushes
forward.

Needle at the sea bottom
78 Shift weight back to right
leg. Right hand pokes downward. Left hand is at left side,
palm down.

47

Fan through the back
79 Step out with left leg. Raise right arm next to head. Left hand follows its motion upward.

80 Shift weight forward, pushing forward with left hand. Right hand stays positioned next to head.

Chop opponent with fist
81 Turn 180 degrees to right. Right hand drops down to waist level in fist position. Left arm follows body movement in a blocking action.

85 Pull back diagonally to left, using waist action.

86 Right foot takes a twisting step forward. Left hand circles to position level with left ear.

Parry
87 Left foot steps forward. At same time, left hand moves forward in parry position.

82   Right backfist.

83   Shift weight forward, pushing with left hand. Right fist is withdrawn to right side.

Step forward parry and punch
84   Turn body 45 degrees to right, reaching forward with right grabbing fist.

88   Shift weight forward to left leg. Punch with right fist. Left hand is positioned opposite the right elbow.

Left ward off
89   Open hands slightly to left ward off position.

Grasp bird's tail
90   Scoop under hand position, right hand protecting lower body, left hand protecting upper body. Left foot steps forward.

Ward off
91 Right hand comes up to
ward off position. Left hand
positioned opposite right elbow.

Roll back
92 Turn waist 45 degrees to
right, reversing palm positions at
the same time.

93 Roll back diagonally, using
waist action.

97 Draw back.

98 Push forward, using hip
power.

Single whip
99 Turn 180 degrees to left.

Press
94   Shift weight back to left leg. Center hips forward. Place left palm on right pulse point.

95   Shift weight forward, using hip power.

Push
96   Straighten arms, keeping elbows slightly bent.

100 Draw right hand back to whip position, with left hand protecting at the right armpit. Look in the direction of the whip hand, but not at the hand.

101 Step out to single whip. Left hand pushes straight ahead.

Wave hands like clouds
102 Shift weight to the right leg, drop the left hand down in a circular motion.

103 Turn the waist to the left, shifting the body weight to the left foot. As the weight shifts left, the left hand circles to a position in front of the face, palm facing the face. The right hand protects the lower body.

104 Right foot closes with the left. Shift body weight to the right foot, while turning the waist to the right. Right hand circles to front of face.

105 Step out with the left foot. Shift body weight to the left foot. Turn waist to left. Left hand circles to front of face.

109 Step out to single whip. Left hand pushes straight ahead.

High pat on horse
110 Shift weight back to right foot. Right hand starts pushing forward.

111 Completion of high pat on horse. Right hand extends forward with hand angled upward. Left hand positioned with palm upward in front of waist.

106 Right foot closes with the left. Shift body weight to the right foot, while turning the waist to the right. Right hand circles to front of face.

107 Step out with the left foot. Shift weight to the left foot. Turn waist to left. Left hand circles to front of face.

Single whip
108 Draw right hand back to whip position, with left hand protecting at the right armpit. Look in the direction of the whip hand.

Separation of right foot
112 Step out diagonally 45 degrees to left. Look toward right.

113 Cross hands and prepare to kick with right foot.

114 Separate hands, keeping both elbow slightly bent. Kick to right corner with right toe.

Separate of left foot
115 Step down diagonally 45 degrees to right. Look to left.

116 Cross hands and prepare to kick with left foot.

117 Separate hands, keeping both elbows slightly bent. Kick to left corner with left toe.

Right brush knee and twist step
121 Turn waist 45 degrees to left and step forward with right foot. Left arm follows direction of waist. Left hand circles to ear level.

122 Right hand brushes down over right knee, while left hand pushes forward.

Step forward and punch downward
123 Step forward with left foot. Left hand brushes down over left knee, while right hand punches downward.

Turn and kick with left sole
118 Pivot on right foot 135
degrees to left. With left foot still
raised from previous kick,
prepare to kick with left heel.

119 Open arms and kick with
left heel.

Left brush knee and twist step
120 Step forward with left foot.
Left hand brushes down over left
knee, while right hand pushes
forward.

Chop opponent with fist
124 Turn 180 degrees to right.
Right hand drops down to waist
level in fist position. Left arm
follows body movement in a
blocking action.

125 Right backfist.

126 Shift weight forward,
pushing with left hand. Right fist
is withdrawn to right side.

Step forward parry and punch
127 Turn body 45 degrees to
right, reaching forward with right
grabbing fist.

128 Pull back diagonally to left,
using waist action.

129 Right foot takes a twisting
step forward. Left hand circles to
position level with left ear.

133 Hands circle into a prepare-
to-kick position.

134 Kick with the right heel.
Both hands spread apart equally.

Hit tiger left
135 Step down with feet
together, right hand extended to
right in a fist. Left hand in fist
position at right elbow.

Parry
130 Left foot steps forward. At same time, left hand moves forward in parry position.

131 Shift weight forward to left leg. Punch with right fist. Left hand is positioned opposite the right elbow.

Kick with right sole
132 Both hands open equally.

136 Step out 45 degrees to left. Right fist crosses in front of face, then drops to waist level. Left fist circles upward to position opposite eyebrows.

Hit tiger right
137 Drop both hands down, while shifting weight to right foot.

138 Shift weight back to left foot, turning body 45 degrees to right.

139 Right foot steps out, Right fist circles upward to position level with eyebrows. Left fist stays at waist level.

Kick with right sole
140 Shift weight back to left foot. Cross arms preparing to kick.

141 Kick with right heel.

145 Kick with left heel.

Turn and kick with right sole
146 Pivot 180 degrees to right.

147 Continue turning 180 degrees to prepare for kick position.

Strike ears with double fist
142 Pivot 45 degrees to right corner. Keep knee up. Drop hands to position parallel with right knee.

143 Step forward with right leg. Hands reach forward to double knuckle strike to temple.

Kick with left sole
144 Shift weight to right leg. Cross hands, preparing to kick.

148 Kick with right heel.

Step forward parry and punch
149 Step down, pulling back with the right hand.

150 Right foot takes a twisting step forward. At same time, left hand moves forward in parry position.

151 Right foot steps forward. At same time, left hand moves forward in parry position.

152 Shift weight forward to left leg. Punch with right fist. Left hand is positioned opposite the right elbow.

Apparent close up
153 Turn right palm upward. Left hand slides forward under right arm.

Cross hands
157 Turn 90 degrees to right.

158 Close hands, right hand on outside. Feet shoulder-width apart.

Carry tiger to the mountain
159 Turn 45 degrees to right. Left hand circles to position next to ear.

154

155 Draw back.

156 Push forward, using hip power.

160 Step out diagonally with right foot. Right hand brushes down over right knee. Left hand pushes forward.

161 Shift weight to left leg. Right hand scoops upward.

162 Shift weight forward to right leg. Right hand chops diagonally to imaginary opponent's throat.

Diagonal grasp bird's tail
163 Roll back, using waist
action.

164 Press forward, placing left
palm against right wrist.

165

Horizontal single whip
169 Turn left 135 degrees,
pivoting on the right heel.

170 Shift weight to right foot,
drawing left foot back to cat
stance position. Draw hands past
body, with right hand in whip
position, left hand protecting next
to the left armpit. Look in the
direction of the whip hand.

171 Step forward to horizontal
single whip, pushing forward with
the left hand.

166 Straighten both hands.

167 Draw back.

168 Push forward, using hip power.

Right partition the wild horse's mane
172 Turn right 90 degrees. Hands close together, right hand protecting the lower body, left hand protecting the upper body.

173 Step forward with the right leg, opening both hands outward at the same time.

Left partition the wild horse's mane
174 Turn the right toe outward 45 degrees, turning the body with it, and close hands with the left hand on the bottom.

175 Step forward with the left leg, opening both hands at the same time.

Right partition the wild horse's mane
176 Turn the left toe outward 45 degrees, turning the body with it, and close hands with the right hand on the bottom.

177 Step forward with the right leg, opening both hands at the same time.

Ward off
181 Right hand comes up to ward off position. Left hand positioned opposite right elbow.

Roll back
182 Turn waist 45 degrees to right, reversing palm positions at the same time.

183 Roll back diagonally, using waist action.

Left ward off
178-179 Step out to the left, approximately 90 degrees, to a left ward off position.

179

Grasp bird's tail
180 Scoop under hand position, right hand protecting lower body, left hand protecting upper body. Left foot steps forward.

Press
184 Shift weight back to left leg. Center hips forward. Place left palm on right pulse point.

185 Shift weight forward, using hip power.

Push
186 Straighten arms, keeping elbows slightly bent.

187 Draw back.

188 Push forward, using hip power.

Single whip
189 Turn 180 degrees to left.

193 Step forward with the left foot. Left hand blocks upward.

194 As the body weight shifts forward to the left foot, the left hand finishes its upward block. Right hand pushes straight.

Left fair lady works the shuttle
195 Close hands, right hand on the bottom. Pivot 315 degrees to right on left foot.

190 Draw right hand back to whip position, with left hand protecting at the right armpit. Look in the direction of the whip hand.

191 Step out to single whip. Left hand pushes straight ahead.

Right fair lady works the shuttle
192 Turn 135 degrees to right, dropping left hand down. Right foot takes a small twist step forward.

196 Step out with right foot. Right hand blocks upward.

Left fair lady works the shuttles
197 As weight is shifted forward, right arm finishes its upward block. Left hand pushes straight.

Right fair lady works the shuttles
198 Pivot on right heel 90 degrees to left. Right hand drops to side.

199 Step out with left foot, blocking upward with left arm, and pushing straight with right hand.

Left fair lady works the shuttles
200 Close hands, right arm on bottom. Pivot 135 degrees to right.

201 Step forward with right leg, blocking upward with the right arm.

Grasp bird's tail
205 Scoop under hand position, right hand protecting lower body, left hand protecting upper body. Left foot steps forward.

Ward off
206 Right hand comes up to ward off position. Left hand positioned opposite right elbow.

Roll back
207 Turn waist 45 degrees to right, reversing palm positions at the same time.

68

202 As weight is shifted forward, right arm finishes its upward block. Left hand pushes straight.

Left ward off
203 Step out 45 degrees to left.

204 Left hand in ward off position.

208 Roll back diagonally, using waist action.

Press
209 Shift weight back to left leg. Center hips forward. Place left palm on right wrist's pulse point.

210 Shift weight forward, using hip power.

Push
211 Straighten arms, keeping elbows slightly bent.

212 Draw back.

213 Push forward, using hip power.

Wave hands like clouds
217 Shift weight to right leg, drop the left hand down in a circular motion.

218 Turn the waist to the left, shifting the body weight to the left foot. As the weight shifts left, the left hand circles to a position in front of the face. The right hand protects the lower body.

219 Right foot closes with the left. Shift body weight to the right foot, while turning the waist to the right. Right hand circles to front of face.

Single whip
214 Turn 180 degrees to left.

215 Draw right hand back to whip position, with left hand protecting at the right armpit. Look in the direction of the whip hand.

216 Step out to single whip. Left hand pushes straight ahead.

220 Step out with left foot. Shift body weight to the left foot. Turn waist to left. Left hand circles to front of face.

221 Right foot closes with the left. Shift body weight to the right foot, while turning waist to right. Right hand circles to front of face.

222 Step out with the left foot. Shift weight to the left foot. Turn waist to left. Left hand circles to front of face.

Single whip
223 Draw right hand back to whip position, with left hand protecting at the right armpit. Look in the direction of the whip hand.

224 Step out to single whip. Left hand pushes straight ahead.

Snake creeps down
225 Shift weight back to right leg. Left arm and hand follow the body's backward movement. Keep the left knee slightly bent.

Right repulse monkey
229 Pick up left foot. Turn left palm upward. Right hand circles to position level with ear.

230 Left foot steps back. Left hand withdraws, as right hand pushes forward.

Left repulse monkey
231 Pick up right foot. Turn right palm upward. Left hand circles to position level with ear.

Right golden rooster stands on one leg
226 Shift the body weight forward, with the right hand following along the centerline.

227 Raise the right leg, toe pointing down. The right arm is poised directly over the right knee.

Left golden rooster stands on one leg
228 Right leg steps back. Raise left leg, toe pointing down. The left arm is poised directly over the left knee.

232 Right foot steps back. Right hand withdraws, as left hand pushes forward.

Right repulse monkey
233 Pick up left foot. Turn left palm upward. Right hand circles to position level with ear.

234 Left foot steps back. Left hand withdraws, as right hand pushes forward.

Slanting flying
235 Turn 90 degrees to right.
Right hand scooped under left
hand.

236 Step out with right foot.
Right hand extends forward.

Raise hands and step forward
237 Shift weight back to left leg.
Right arm extends forward. Left
hand positioned opposite right
elbow.

241 Right hand pushes up to
the front. Left hand pushes
down. Pick up left foot, replacing
it with the toe down, heel up.

Left brush knee and twist step
242 Turn right arm inward, palm
toward the face. Lower right
hand, while raising left hand.

243 Raise left hand to shoulder
level. Turn waist 45 degrees to
right. Left hand follows direction
of waist 45 degrees to right. Left
hand follows direction of waist.
Right hand circles to position at
ear level.

Stork spreads its wings
238 Pull back with both hands,
using waist action.

239 Scoop under, right hand
protecting lower body and left
hand protecting upper body.

240 Step out with right foot into
a right shoulder strike.

244 Step forward with left foot.
Left hand brushes down over left
knee, as right hand pushes
forward.

Needle at sea bottom
245 Shift weight back to right
leg. Right hand pokes downward. Left hand is at left side,
palm down.

Fan through the back
246 Step out with left leg. Raise
right arm next to head. Left hand
follows its motion.

247 Shift weight forward, pushing forward with left hand. Right hand stays positioned next to head.

White snake puts out its tongue
248 Turn 180 degrees to right. Right hand drops down to waist level in open hand position. Left arm follows body movement in a blocking action.

249 Right back of the hand strike.

Parry
253 Left foot steps forward. At same time, left hand moves forward in parry position.

254 Shift weight forward to left leg. Punch with right fist. Left hand is positioned opposite the right elbow.

Left ward off
255 Open hands slightly to left ward off position.

250 Shift weight forward, pushing with left hand. Right hand is withdrawn to the right side.

Step forward parry and punch
251 Turn body 45 degrees to right, reaching forward with right grabbing fist. Pull back diagonally to left, using waist action.

252 Right foot takes a twisting step forward. At same time, left hand moves forward in parry position.

Grasp bird's tail
256 Scoop under hand position, right hand protecting lower body, left hand protecting upper body. Left foot steps forward.

Ward off
257 Right hand comes up to ward off position. Left hand positioned opposite right elbow.

Roll back
258 Turn waist 45 degrees to right, reversing palm positions at the same time.

259 Roll back diagonally, using waist action.

Press
260 Shift weight back to left leg. Center hips forward. Place left palm on right pulse point.

261 Shift weight forward, using hip power.

Single whip
265 Turn 180 degrees to left.

266 Draw right hand back to whip position, with left hand protecting at the right armpit. Look in the direction of the whip hand.

267 Step out to single whip. Left hand pushes straight ahead.

Push
262 Straighten arms, keeping elbows slightly bent.

263 Draw back.

264 Push forward, using hip power.

Wave hands like clouds
268 Shift weight to the right leg, drop the left hand down in a circular motion.

269 Turn the waist to the left, shifting the body weight to the left foot. As the weight shifts left, the left hand circles to a position in front of the face. The right hand protects the lower body.

270 Right foot closes with the left, shifting body weight to the right foot, while turning the waist to the right. Right hand circles to front of face.

271 Step out with the left foot. Shift body weight to the left foot. Turn waist to left. Left hand circles to front of face.

272 Right foot closes with the left. Shift body weight to the right foot, while turning the waist to the right. Right hand circles to front of face.

273 Step out with the left foot. Shift weight to the left foot. Turn waist to left. Left hand circles to front of face.

277 Completion of high pat on horse. Right hand extends forward with hand angled upward. Left hand positioned with palm upward in front of waist.

Plain crossed hands
278 Left elbow crosses right hand diagonally.

Turn and cross-kick
279 Turn 180 degrees to right. Left arm blocks across.

Single whip
274 Draw right hand back to
whip position, with left hand
protecting at the right armpit.
Look in the direction of the whip
hand.

275 Step out to single whip. Left
hand pushes straight ahead.

High pat on horse
276 Shift weight back to right
foot. Right hand starts pushing
forward.

280 Cross arms, right arm on
outside.

281 Outward cross-kick, using
right hand as target.

Brush knee and punch low
282 Pull back with right fist,
using waist action.

283 Right foot makes a twisting step forward. Left hand circles to position level with ear.

284 Left foot steps forward. Left hand continues down in brush knee position.

285 Punch low with the right fist.

Roll back
289 Turn waist 45 degrees to right, reversing palm positions at the same time.

290 Roll back diagonally, using waist action.

Press
291 Shift weight back to left leg. Center hips forward. Place left palm on right pulse point.

Left ward off
286 Step out to the left to a
ward off position.

Grasp bird's tail
287 Scoop under hand position,
right hand protecting lower body,
left hand protecting upper body.
Right foot steps forward.

Ward off
288 Right hand comes up to
ward off position. Left hand
positioned opposite right elbow.

292 Shift weight forward, using
hip power.

Push
293 Draw back, with arms apart.

294 Push forward, using hip
power.

Single whip
295 Turn 180 degrees to left.

296 Draw back right hand to whip position, with left hand protecting at the right armpit. Look in the direction of the whip hand.

297 Step out to single whip. Left hand pushes straight ahead.

Step back to ride a tiger
301 Step back with right leg. Left heel up, weight on right leg. Separate hands, with right hand protecting head, left hand at left side next to thigh.

Lotus kick
302 Drop right hand down. Bring left hand up, above the right arm.

303 Pivot on right foot 180 degrees to right.

Snake creeps down
298 Shift weight back to right leg. Left arm and hand follow the body's backward movement. Keep the left knee slightly bent.

Step up to seven star
299 Make a fist with the left hand. Shift the weight onto the left leg. Right hand in fist position at right side.

300 Step forward with right leg, heel up, weight on left leg. Right arm crosses under left arm. Both hands are fists.

304 Place weight on left leg, turning body another 180 degrees to right. Bring both arms to right side.

305 Lotus kick to right (crescent kick to right).

Shoot a tiger
306 Place right foot down at 45-degree angle to right corner. Both hands on left side.

307 Shift weight to right foot. Drop both hands down, carrying them over to right side, left fist at right armpit and right fist next to right ear.

308 Punch 45 degrees to left corner with right fist. Left fist draws slightly back.

Step forward parry and punch 309 Shift weight to left foot, pulling back with right hand.

Apparent close-up 313-314 Left hand slides forward under right arm. Turn right palm upward.

314

315 Draw back.

86

310 Right foot takes a twisting step forward. At same time, left hand circles to position next to left ear.

311 Left foot steps forward, left hand moves forward to parry position.

312 Shift weight forward to left leg. Punch with right fist. Left hand is positioned opposite right elbow.

316 Push forward, using hip power.

Cross hands
317 Turn 90 degrees to right.

318 Close hands, right hand on outside. Feet a shoulder's-distance apart.

Conclusion
319-320 Hands come down to
sides. At same time, stand up.

320

321 Left foot closes with right.

Chapter Six –
Correct Form Practice

Tai chi is a scientific martial art. If you don't follow the principles, the result is poor tai chi. Each principle is structured around precise body actions, incorporating different angles and directions. There is no question that good tai chi comes through hard work and correct practice. If you do not correctly practice the form, you will never reach your full potential in tai chi push hand practice.

The external appearance of tai chi form techniques, postures and footwork must be correct. This *external* appearance is how you position your arms and legs when you move. As a rule, correct form is also nice-looking form, but with tai chi there's more to it than just beauty.

Once you learn the form and memorize its sequence, you must work on keeping five parts of your body *down*. From top to bottom, those five areas are the shoulders, chest, elbows, hips and back heel.

Shoulders

In tai chi chuan practice, your shoulders are always down and relaxed. When your shoulders are raised they cause your chest muscles to tense, making your breathing rise in the chest cavity.

Shoulders raised – Incorrect.

For martial art purposes, people with tense, raised shoulders are easily thrown off balance, because their bodies are too stiff. When your shoulders are tense, your striking energy is broken at the shoulder joint. This seriously restricts your power and force. This is illustrated through accounts of old tai chi masters in China throwing people across a room with no apparent effort.

Elbow

Keep your elbows down. If the elbows are raised sideways, any striking or defending arm leverage is weak. In close-range grappling situations, raised elbows make it easy for someone to put you into an arm or shoulderlock. By raising your elbow sideways, you've already accomplished half the jointlock, making it easy for your opponent to finish his task.

Raised elbows also make your shoulders stiff and chest muscles tense, causing you to breathe high in the chest.

One way to check your elbow position is to raise your hands in front with your palms facing you as if you were holding a mirror in each palm. Keep your elbows straight down. Then turn your palms outward into a pushing position, without moving the elbows. Your elbow position is now correct.

90

Elbows – incorrect – raised.

Elbows – correct – elbows dropped.

Chest

Don't stand in any tai chi posture with your chest sticking out, as though you were a soldier standing at attention. Your chest should always be relaxed and slightly concave.

Correct breathing is another reason for keeping your chest muscles relaxed. Most people only use the upper third of their lung capacity when they breathe. The accepted goal for both martial arts and health is to use your full lung capacity and breathe deeply into the lower

Chest – incorrect – chest raised.

Chest – correct – relaxed.

abdomen. To that end, you cannot have tense chest muscles and expect to breathe with your entire lung capacity.

A relaxed chest is important to martial artists, because if your chest sticks out, your back is swayed. This means your upper and lower back lacks strength because it's no longer connected. If your chest is relaxed, it is easier for your breathing and chi to move down into your tan tian.

Why is this important for martial artists?

When you only breathe in the upper part of your chest, your upper body is too heavy and your lower extremities are too light, which may throw you off balance. Also, breathing too high in the chest causes the heel of your back to come off the ground. This makes it easy for people to pull or push you off balance.

Hips and Waist

No matter what style of tai chi you practice, your hips should *always* be tucked, with your pelvis turned upward. If your hips stick out to the rear, your back is swayed and there is no body connection. This leads to little power and balance.

Any martial artist should take full advantage of the *ming men* pressure point and its resulting lower back energy. Chinese traditional medical practitioners believe that the ming men–the pressure point directly opposite the navel–is as important as the tan tian energy

Waist – incorrect – too tense, with hip joint pushed forward.

Waist – correct – waist and hip joint relaxed.

source, located three fingers below the navel. A look at an anatomy chart shows a large mass of nerves–serving the lower back, abdominal organs, and the lower extremities–surrounding the ming men. This is a critical nerve mass, especially regarding strength coming from the hips and back. For maximum strength and health benefits you should curve your tailbone inward, straightening, instead of swaying, your lower back.

Your waist should be relaxed and flexible; a flexible waist makes your lower body foundation stronger by letting you position your feet in their strongest natural position. It is also easier to control and maximize the weight distribution over your center of gravity. Waist action, combined with a straight back, determines the connection between upper and lower body.

Back Foot

When practicing tai chi, your back foot and heel must remain flat on the ground. A common mistake with tai chi practitioners is turning the back foot's heel or pulling the side of the foot off the ground. Your feet must be flat before they are rooted and stable.

Whenever any part of your back foot is off the ground, it is easy to mistakenly turn your knee inward. It's also easier for you to lean too far forward, pushing the knee on your front leg well over your toe. By carrying your energy down the side of your back ankle, your foot will stay flat.

Now that you know the five parts of your body to keep down, here are a few more pointers on correct tai chi forms.

Back – correct – straight, with hips tucked forward.

Back – incorrect – buttocks stick out, lower back swayed.

93

Back – incorrect – leaning too far forward.

Back – correct – straight.

Back – incorrect – leaning too far forward.

Position your head as if a thread is attached to its top. Always look straight at your imaginary target. Holding your head upright and looking straight ahead keeps your energy moving forward, and helps chi flow and visual focus. Yang Cheng-Fu wrote, "Your intention is to slightly push your head upward. However, do not use too much concentration and strength. If your do, your neck becomes stiff. Your head position should be natural, using only a small amount of intention. If you don't hold your head correctly, your spirit is not alert."

Keep your back straight, with your weight directly over your center of gravity for correct balance. Don't make the mistake of judging someone's or your own back position by the illusion created by loose clothing. You should feel whether your back is straight by the line from neck to tailbone.

Don't let your shoulder blades protrude. Your shoulders should be slightly rounded, but not stooped. With your shoulders relaxed and rounded, place your chi intention along the length of your back. Imagine you are pushing your internal energy into your back. If you do this your strength and energy will come from your back, rather than just your arms and shoulders. Yesterday's tai chi masters all said that real strength comes primarily from the spine.

When your hand extends forward in a pushing position, your arm should appear straight, but not straight. In other words, there is a very slight bend to your elbow that makes it look bent but not bent. Don't push with a straight arm and locked elbow joint. If you actually push or hit something, you will injure your elbow joint.

Keep your upper arm away from your ribcage, bringing it in close only when punching forward. If you keep it an inch or two away from your ribs, you have better resistance against a push to that arm. You have little resistance when your arm is positioned against your body. Always make sure that your elbows stay down.

As you know, the wrist joins your hand to your arm. If your wrist has no intention in its positioning, your palm will drop down like a

Correct hand position.

Correct palm energy.

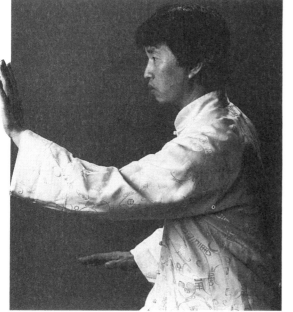

dead rose. The neck of a rose without water droops. Add water and it comes back to life. When your wrist hangs like a drooping rose, it's because you have no intention in your hand and wrist action. In an actual fighting situation, a person could easily break your wrist if you have no energy in the hand. However, if you bend the wrist too much, it will stop the circulation of energy and strength into the palm. Correct wrist position should be the same as holding your hands against a wall, elbows down, without tensing your wrists. Try this, then step back and check your hand position. This principle applies to the push, single whip, fair lady, brush knee, and repulse monkey tai chi techniques.

When you move, use intention, not physical strength for power. In an actual fighting situation, power comes from a combination of body mass times speed of movement. Therefore, when you practice tai chi, your body must be loose and relaxed. Use absolutely no tense force. Once your muscles tense, even slightly, your chi circulation gets stuck in those muscles.

But you might ask, "If you don't use any strength, how can you develop force?"

In the body, chi meridians might be compared to a drainage system. If the drain isn't blocked, water will flow. It's the same with our bodies. When the chi meridians are not blocked, chi will move. If your body is tense with stiff strength, your chi and blood circulation are disturbed and blocked. When muscles are tense, movements are slower. Without speed behind your body mass, there's little power. Your best speed is produced by relaxed muscles.

When you just use intention-directing movement, your chi is directed by your intention, and your blood directed by your chi. That leads to proper body circulation.

Practice relaxation and intention long enough, and you will develop real inner energy. One old tai chi chuan book says if you can reach extremely soft practice, you will later produce extremely hard techniques. The book also says that good tai chi practitioners have arms that are like cotton wrapped around steel–soft but very heavy.

Another must for correct tai chi practice is palm energy. Both palms should stay relaxed, with your fingers naturally spread. Don't let your fingers curl. Too limp or too stiff also is not correct. Correct palm and finger position is similar to putting your hand out and asking for something.

Eye position is a critical part of correct tai chi practice. Remember, tai chi is a martial art. Don't practice it with a mindless, unfocused

Demonstration of empty and full footwork. Right foot is empty, while left foot is full.

gaze. You eyes should look straight in the direction of your imaginary target. Your eyes *follow* your hand's direction, but should never directly look at the hand. Looking at the hand is a common mistake. Your eyes should look at the attacking hand's *direction*.

What Chinese call *shen* (spirit) also is very important. Think of your shen as the general and your body as the soldier. If you have a strong spirit, then your body moves light and lively. Shen directs the body.

Keep your body level when moving from posture to posture. Don't bob up and down. Bobbing leads to weak balance and foundation. You cannot deliver power if your body is moving up and down as much as forward.

The only technique that drops the body lower than its usual position is the snake creeps down posture. In our Yang style, the stork spreads its wings position is an upright posture, standing slightly taller than the other techniques. All other movements should stay at the same level throughout the form.

Timing also is an important part of tai chi practice. On a martial art level, timing is essential; if your reaction time is off, you'll likely miss your target. Although tai chi is practiced slowly, timing is developed into a subconscious habit by keeping everything even and at the same speed. Consider all tai chi movements like pulling a silk thread from a cocoon–soft and even–being careful not to break the thread with jerky movements.

Your footwork is closely related to timing. Old tai chi masters refer to correct footwork as being *empty and full*, rather than *double weighted*. As your weight shifts from one foot to another, one becomes full and the other empty. Double weighted is an undesirable situation, where both feet carry almost equal amounts of body weight. From a double-weighted position it is difficult to move and quickly change directions. People moving while double weighted have their center of gravity split into two uneven divisions. This reduces their stability. They are stiff, heavy and awkward. Your weight and center of gravity should completely shift from one foot to the other before you initiate another movement.

When you understand the theory of empty and full footwork, you can quickly shift in all directions with lively, well-balanced footwork.

If correctly done, your moving steps are similar to a cat. A cat steps so lightly, it doesn't make sound. When you move the same way–light and relaxed–you advance and retreat easily and quickly in fighting situations.

Moving isn't everything in tai chi. Equally as important are the stationary stances. An example of a correct tai chi stance is the common *bow and arrow* stance. Your forward knee should not extend beyond the toe of the same foot. If it does, you are putting too much stress on your knee and will probably develop sore knees. Your toe should turn 15 degrees inward for stability.

The knee of your back leg should be slightly bent, helping your back remain straight. If the knee of your back leg is bent too much, your knee will turn inward and the back of your foot may come off the ground. Keep 60 percent of your weight over the front foot and the remainder over the back foot. Before moving, shift your weight over your stationary foot, preventing double weightedness. While still in the bow and arrow stance, slightly open your legs and concentrate on expanding your energy in all directions. According to ancient tai chi chuan classics, your upper and lower body follow each other. In other words, motion starts from the feet. Energy is first released through the legs, controlled by the waist, and manifested through the fingers. All motion from the feet to the leg to the waist simultaneously acts together, leading to the old tai chi saying, "All motion starts at the same time and finishes at the same time." When your hand moves, your waist and foot also move. Even your eyes move with the rest of the motion. When this is done, your upper and lower body automatically connect. If one body part isn't in action with the others, your power connection and flow is broken.

Tai chi differs from other, more external martial arts because its movement is continuous and unbroken. Other martial arts use strength that is basically physical action with a stop-and-go type energy. The disadvantage comes when your opponent catches you at the point in your timing when the old strength is finished and the new strength hasn't started its cycle. That's the time when he easily throws you off guard and off balance.

In tai chi we use *yi* (intention) and even timing, combined with relaxed physical strength. From beginning to end there is a cycle of continuous recirculated energy and movement.

Since many martial artists from other systems use only broken physical strength, they find themselves puffing and out of breath after a sparring match or long form. Good tai chi practitioners know to take their time and relax, especially when fighting external stylists. They wait until the external martial artist is tired, then get him with relaxed tai chi principles. This was called *calm waiting for action* by ancient tai chi experts. When practicing tai chi forms, do them slow and even. Then your breathing goes deep and low in your abdomen, taking your chi down with it. The ancients called this *action seeking calm*. Practice the form to learn relaxation and calmness. When you fight you are calmer and more relaxed than your opponent. This helps conserve energy.

Demonstration of open.   Demonstration of close.

The tai chi form itself is based on *empty and full* and *open and close*. You know what empty and full represents. Let's look at open and close. Open is seen in techniques such as *partition the wild horse's mane*. In that posture, not only do your hands and legs spread open, your mind and intention should push chi outward. The opposite, close, is a closing movement, such as in *cross hands*. It also is the result of your mind and intention bringing chi closer to your body.

In terms of sheer strength, chi gives you expanding energy when you push or punch. This is *open* energy. Chi also gives you extra contracting energy when you need to pull your opponent closer. That is *closing* energy.

There are some portions of tai chi practice that defy conventional explanations. You'll find the answers only after you've practiced correct basics over a long time.

Here are a few translations from tai chi classics you must experience before you understand.

• Using power is not right. No strength is also not right. Soft carrying hard is right.

• Losing contact is not right. Forcing is not right. Not losing, not tensing is right.

• Adhesive is not right. Not adhesive is not right. Not leaving and not forcing is right.

• Light is not right. Heavy is not right. Loose and heavy is right.

• Too much aggressiveness is not right. No aggressiveness is not right. Courage carrying caution is right.

• Hitting people is not right. Not hitting people is not right. Having their respect is right. (Use a technique that doesn't hurt them, but shows your power.)

These are the secrets to advanced tui shou–push hands. You must understand the tai chi form before you understand these principles.

Chapter Seven –
Practical Applications
of Form Techniques

Raise hands – a lifting elbowlock.

Partition the wild horse's mane – An upper body strike and push, using waist motion.

Stork spreads its wings – Stopping a fist and kicking
attack, while preparing for a countering kick.

Brush knee and twist step – Simultaneously blocking and
kicking and countering with a straight push.

Repulse monkey – Escaping a grab with one hand, while striking to the throat with the other.

Needle at the sea bottom – Countering a wrist grab with a wristlock and takedown.

Rollback – A shoulder lock, using the waist for leverage.

Press – Straight push.

Elbow over fist – An elbow strike to the back of the neck.

High pat on horse – A strike to the jaw, while holding one of the opponent's arms down.

Golden rooster stands on one leg – Deflecting a punch with one hand, while kicking to the opponent's groin.

Lotus kick – A cross-kick to the back, while pulling the opponent backward into the kick.

Punch down – A downward punch to the face of a prone opponent.

Hit tiger – A fist strike to the side of the head, while holding one arm down.

Double strike with the fist – A double knuckle strike to the opponent's temples.

Separation of left toe – A simultaneous block and kick to the groin.

Fair lady works the shuttles – A simultaneous upward block and straight push.

Parry and punch – A deflecting block and punch to the body.

Fan through the back – An upward block and push to the body. Note: the block can also be a grab.

Plain cross-hands – A finger jab to the throat, while pressing down with the blocking hand.

Chapter Eight –
Tai Chi Push Hands

Tai chi *tui shou*, or *push hands* are as important to tai chi, the martial art, as meditation, stances, or form practice.

It has been said that practicing the form teaches you to know *yourself*, while push hands let you know your *opponent*. There's nothing mystical in this statement. It simply means that when you correctly practice forms, you are teaching your body to relax and react in its most mechanically efficient manner as a single connected force.

Push hands practice teaches you to feel your opponent's strong and weak points, instantly knowing where you should attack or defend. Eventually, when your push hands are developed well enough, you will know your opponent's next move or weakness as soon as you touch hands or arms with him. Push hands is the sparring part of tai chi.

Although push hands gives you an opportunity to try out your many faceted tai chi training under sparring circumstances, don't expect to start with the freestyle version. First you must become familiar with shou patterns, developing your sensitivity and what the Chinese call *listening* ability.

The most common pattern in Yang tai chi is a double-hand pattern, where each person alternates defense and offense by exchanging a smoothly moving pattern from one person to another. However, this two-handed push hand pattern is not easily learned. It's better to start with a single hand tui shou pattern that develops sensitivity, continuity and relaxation.

Single-Hand Push Hands
Start with say, the right leg one leg forward. Your weight should rest over your left leg, with the leg pointed 45 degrees forward. For stability turn your right foot inward about 15 degrees. Place your right arm into a ward-off position, lightly touching your opponent's right arm, which is also in a ward-off position. You and your opponent have the right legs and right arms forward. You may place your left arm behind your back or out to the side, whichever helps with balance.

You and your partner now exchange attacking and defending postures, waiting for the opportune moment by shifting your weight over your forward foot, while still keeping your spine straight.

When you shift your weight forward, your opponent leans back by moving his weight over the rear leg and sinking his hips to deflect your push. He rotates the waist to the right if he has contact with his right arm and to the left if tui shou is done left arm to left arm. Do not lift the toe of your forward foot when shifting back your weight. Only Wu style tai chi does that.

Then it is your partner's turn to come forward, attacking if he wants. The pattern is a continuous exchange of offensive and defensive movements. Of course, you won't try to push each time you shift forward into attacking position. Wait until you feel a weakness in your opponent's defenses or balance.

Contact between you and your partner is not wrist to wrist. It should be the first third of your *forearm* to the first third of your partner's forearm. This gives both of you more wrist flexibility and a slightly longer reach.

One reason to start with single-hand push hands before double push hands is to develop relaxation and waist action. If your shoulders get sore, you are too tense. The other reason is to learn to *stick*. When your opponent moves, your arm should move with him and never lose contact. If you break contact, you create a weakness in your own defenses and allow the opponent to use sudden force against you.

Practice single push hands equally on both sides.

Single push hands pattern
Ward-off position.

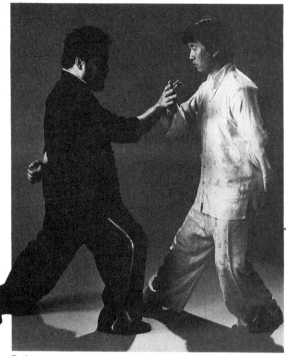

Defend by withdrawing and deflecting the opponent's
forward momentum.

Push forward.

The opponent defends.

114

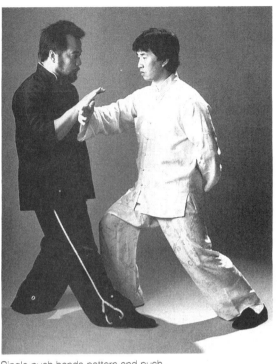

Single push hands pattern and push .

Double Push Hands

When you are comfortable doing single push hands, you can start practicing the double tui shou pattern with a partner. Place your right arm up in a ward-off position. It makes no difference which leg is forward, only that if your right foot is forward; your partner's right foot also should be forward.

Your partner will place both hands on your ward off arm, in a pushing position–the right hand on your wrist and the left on your elbow. Now he pushes forward. Place your left arm inside your right arm in the same ward-off position, and exchange it for your right arm, creating a *bridge* between your chest and your partner's pushing hands.

Drop your right arm down and around in a half-circle to a position with the palm against your partner's left elbow. Push your partner's left arm up, by pushing against his left elbow and wrist, using your right hand against his left wrist. You are now in the attacking position, ready to push forward against your partner's ward off arm.

Repeat with your pushing and your partner defending as you just did. In this direction, you are defending with your right arm and your partner with the left arm. When you become adept at this direction, smoothly change directions by simply reversing the pushing direction. After changing directions, your left arm is the ward off arm, while your partner's right takes on that responsibility.

Reversing directions is a valuable defense tactic against a straight push, redirecting the attacker's force away from you. Don't try double push-hand sparring until you are proficient in both directions.

When you know both single and double push-hands patterns, your training naturally evolves into four distinct stages, each with its own special kind of energy, called jing in Chinese.

The first stage is dong jing, or understanding energy. At this level, you begin to understand the different types of force and resistance used against you. For instance, when someone uses either the neutralizing or discharging force against you, you must recognize and understand its type. Dong jing knowledge is a must before you can move on to the next stage. You may not know how to deflect or neutralize his attack, but you should understand the difference between sticky (nian jing), adhesive (zhan jing), connecting (lian jing) and following (sui jing).

The second stage is called ting jing. It means listening or feeling energy. Ting jing helps you feel how strong or weak, tense or limp your opponent is at the moment of contact. When you develop ting jing, you'll instantly know whether the opponent's elbow is tense or if he's off balance. Well-trained tai chi practitioners feel these sensations through their entire body at the initial touch, as if the opponent were broadcasting on silent radio waves. Ting jing is practical knowledge, used to feel the opponent's intentions and weaknesses.

After ting jing comes *hua jing*, or *dissolving* energy. Hua jing is just what it implies. When people push or attack you, once you make contact you neutralize their forceful jing. Do that by slightly yielding, then redirecting the force. Hua jing requires relaxation and sticking ability. You must learn to follow your opponent's force, using it to your own advantage.

The final stage is *fa jing*. Fa jing is *discharging* or *releasing* energy. After you use hua jing to neutralize and put your opponent off balance, it is your chance to discharge jing. Fa jing is that discharging power and is characterized by sudden explosive force.

Tai chi push hand patterns use four basic fighting tactics within the hua jing and fa jing levels. They are *ward off (peng)*, *roll back (lu)*, *press (ji)*, and *push (an)*.

An example of ward off is: After contact with your opponent's arm during double push-hands practice, both hands and elbows stick together. If you move, your opponent moves. If you don't he doesn't. Ward off is the physical connection that establishes ting jing or listening energy.

Roll back is a *following* action. If someone pushes straight against you, you will turn your waist from your roll back arm, rotating and rolling your arm along his pushing arm as you redirect or deflect the force of his push. In the end you are still balanced, while your opponent is off balance.

Press is an offensive tactic used when you try pulling your opponent or rolling back and your opponent pulls back against your pulling force. At that tensed moment, follow your opponent's movement, pressing the palm of one hand against the inside of the wrist of the other hand. Attack straight forward.

Push is another offensive technique. If your opponent is weak, push straight forward with both hands. For tense opponents, neutralize their push by sticking to their hands, circling downward, and pushing forward.

After double push-hand patterns comes push hands sparring and da lu practice. Don't try freestyle push hands until you are good at pattern tui shou. If you try freestyle sparring too soon, it can easily turn into force against force pushing or wrestling. Da lu, or *great pull*, adds four more techniques to the basic ward off, roll back, press and push. Those four techniques are *cai* (*pull*), *lie* (*bend backward*), *zhou* (*elbow strike*), *kou* (*shoulder strike*).

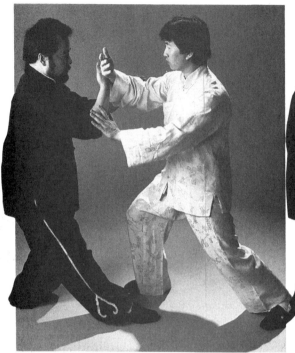

Double push-hands pattern.

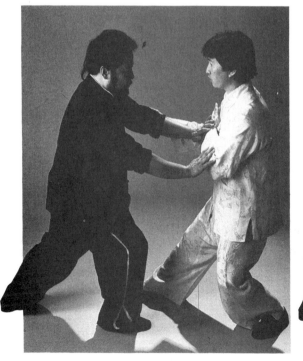

 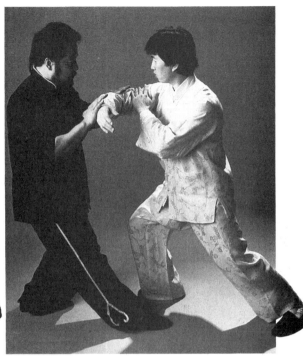

Cai is a sudden downward pull, like jerking someone's arm. Lie is a joint-breaking action that hyperextends the opponent's joint by bending it against its natural direction.

Zhou is used by placing leverage against someone with your elbow, as in a jointlock. It also is a strike that takes the opponent off balance or injures him. Kou is a leaning action or a direct shoulder strike. Leaning against someone is usually done to take him off balance.

Da lu footwork is different from regular pattern push hands. It is footwork that moves diagonally forward and backward in four directions.

Nowadays, push-hand sparring is becoming popular in tournament competition. Some tournaments allow only stationary footwork, others let opponents travel at will within 20-foot circles, using tai chi freestyle sparring tactics.

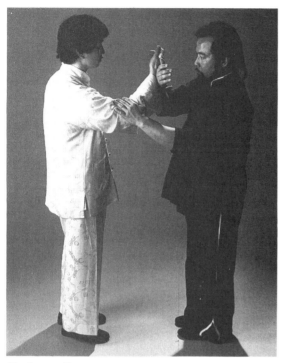

Starting position.

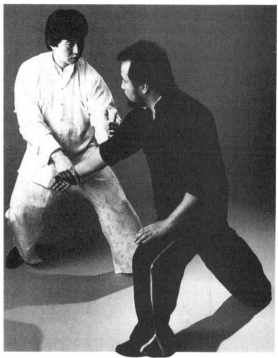

Cai, a straight downward pull, the opponent does *kou*, a shoulder strike.

Lie, leverage against the shoulder joint.

Zhou, an elbow strike.

About the Authors

Doc-Fai Wong

Doc-Fai Wong has been teaching Yang style tai chi chuan and choy li fut kung-fu since 1968 at his headquarters school in San Francisco, Calif. Besides the San Francisco school, he has branches throughout the United States and Europe.

In 1987 he was promoted to grandmaster of the Choy Li Fut/Tai Chi Chuan International Federation by his teacher in Hong Kong, Hu Yuen-Chou, who retired from the position.

Grandmaster Wong represents direct second-generation lineage to Yang Cheng-Fu, the greatest teacher of Yang tai chi. His own teacher, Hu Yuen-Chou, was a close disciple of Yang Cheng-Fu.

Doc-Fai Wong was the coach for the United States team competing in Taiwan in 1987, in the Republic of China International Tai Chi Chuan Federation's World Championship Push Hands competition–an international tournament held every four years. His American team was the first and only U.S. team to win anything at this tournament, placing second to Taiwan in the team standings and winning first, second and third places in individual standings.

In September, 1987, he and Jane Hallander sponsored the first all-tai chi chuan forms and push hands tournament on America's West Coast.

Wong has been featured on the covers of national and foreign martial arts magazines. He is featured in Who's Who in California and Who's Who in American Martial Arts. He is also a monthly columnist for *Inside Kung-Fu* magazine. He is also the author of *Choy Li Fut Kung Fu* and *Shaolin Five Animal Kung Fu*.

Doc-Fai Wong is a California State Certified acupuncturist and herbalist. He is also an expert in *qi gong* (chi kung), being a longtime disciple of professor Peng-Si Yu and Min Ou-Yang, two of China's greatest qi gong teachers.

Jane Hallander

Jane Hallander is one of the world's best-known martial arts writers, having over 300 magazine articles published in the United States and abroad. She is the author of *Guide to Kung Fu Fighting Styles*, *Choy Li Fut Kung Fu*, *The Fighting Weapons of Korean Martial Arts*, *Shaolin Five Animals Kung Fu*, and *Kajukenbo*.

Besides her martial arts journalism, Hallander writes for various newspapers and foreign journals.

When not writing, Hallander spends her time teaching and practicing tai chi chuan. At one time the senior tai chi instructor at Doc-Fai Wong's headquarters school, she now has her own tai chi school in San Rafael, Calif. She has been a student of Doc-Fai Wong since 1979, and makes yearly excursions to Hong Kong for additional corrections from his teacher, Hu Yuen-Chou.

Hallander is a national and international champion in tai chi forms and push hands competitions at both tai chi and open tournaments.

Like her own teacher, Doc-Fai Wong, Jane Hallander is also a qi gong disciple of professor Peng-Si Yu and Min Ou-Yang. She began her qi gong studies in 1982.